Notes from Under the Covers

Waking with Arthritis

Cynthia Tyler

Thanks to Robert Kaleta-Schuetz for the cover photo.

ISBN-10: 1496151445
ISBN-13: 9781496151445
Library of Congress Control Number: 2014904455
CreateSpace Independent Publishing Platform
North Charleston, South Carolina

This book is dedicated to the memory of my maternal grandmother

Ona Mae Stewart Nelson

In the last weeks of her life she spoke of her youth, how by the time she was in eighth grade she really liked to write. I suspect she didn't get a lot farther than that: she was sixteen when my mother was born. But, my grandmother's voice was wistful when she spoke: You know, I thought sometimes maybe I could have been a writer.

Nanny, this one is for you.

Introduction

$\mathcal{I}$ don't know how it started – a pen on the night table, a notebook purchased for some now forgotten purpose, that somehow wound up on the bed. And there I was: arthritis was crippling me, I was often overcome by melancholy (a wonderfully archaic way of saying I was really depressed), forced by pain and hideously overgrown knuckles to quit working as a calligrapher. I was waking to that reality every morning. It wasn't pleasant, and at some point the suffering had to express itself.

A goal was set, to write a poem every morning before I even got out of bed - hence, the 'Under the Covers' reference. For a while it went pretty well. It only fell off when sleep became an unknown state, when the discomfort I felt every morning was far greater than the need to write. Still, it allowed me the joy of the creative experience, the satisfaction of completing an assignment – before even getting out of bed!

You will recognize the poems that deal with the arthritis easily enough. There are some other bits that may have been born from something in the news, or the actions of my cats, memories that stirred as the work that had been my life receded from the day's worries...

We all of us grow older. I knew I would. I knew that, unless I died first, I would get older, and maybe my body wouldn't work so well, and eventually I would stop looking twenty years younger than I am as the first wrinkles made their appearance.

I just didn't think it would be NOW. Eighty-two, of course. Seventy-two, possibly. But in the first years of sixties...it seemed an unbearable sentence. I had spent my life as an artisan, working with hand and eye. Now, the hand was crippled, and the eye developed an untreatable and incurable ailment that would increasingly inhibit my vision. I began to think of it as God's joke.

I can't wait to hear the punchline!.

Since that time, my life has undergone a great change. It became possible for me to get hip replacement surgery, which has given me a new beginning: better health, greater mobility, and hope. Hope is maybe the greatest of the gifts. It is with hope that I compose this little book, publish, and try to sell it. Life is vast and complicated, sometimes beautiful, too often difficult. But everything can change in an instant (or, at least, after two hours of surgery!). My desire for you is that you would never lose hope, and trust that change for the better is always waiting just around the bend.

Suggestions for the reader

*Y*ou will notice something a little different about this book: all of the left side pages have been left blank. If you are reading this volume because you are experiencing the difficulty I had with arthritis, or hip replacement surgery, or just because - well, just because - that left page is there so you can make notes, write comments, jot down your thoughts, start keeping your own diary. The individual poems are indicated by the date of writing, and some days were good, and have more than one poem. You are free to enter your own dates on your entries.

You may even want to paste additions on those blank sheets: an autumn leaf, a photo of yourself, or your cat (or dog or grandchildren), a recipe for chicken soup, a photo of that place you want to visit when you get well. The poems are a sort of diary that I kept for myself during a very difficult time. I hope that the ultimate message will be one of comfort and hope. In the meantime, sometimes it's good to leave your footprints on the path.

$\mathcal{I}$ often wake early enough for the sign-on of NPR's Morning Edition. Here in Atlanta, it starts at five am. With a low volume, the murmur of voices sometimes lulls me back to sleep. But bits and pieces of the headlines still find their way into my brain, and maybe it's not for the best: maintaining optimism in the face of the revolution du jour or the castastrophe of the month is asking a lot. The gift? I learn every morning how very lucky I am.

September 2

Somewhere, perhaps,
is some celestial box
invisable, but dense
with all the horror of those
most ugly souls who
consumed the
lives of others and
dragged a veil of terror
across the earth.
The gross mistakes
of human procreation,
the ones whose wiring
went awry, whose
personal connection
to humanity at large
seems never to have
been aware of its
own existence, of its

necessity to be.
You know the names:
history preserves them.
But dear God,
does no time come
that all who rot
with hatred for their
fellow man will be
at last removed,
locked up in that
heavenly cell
to allow this fragile sphere
to heal?

I use facebook. Many have been there to 'listen' when I was hurting, to help when I was trying to raise funds for my surgery, to rejoice with me at my progress back to good health. Many have also needed me, and I have offered a shoulder, a suggestion, or sympathy as I could. Between us, we share a lot, which offers opportunity for observation and commentary.

September 3

She said she stopped opposing
and it got better.
And she's right.
At least half depression's pain
is because you stand
and try to fight.

Time will pass: you will learn
to know depression's
grasping core.
You'll come to see the sense
of saying 'Welcome, friend'
and let it through the door.

It seems to need a kindness
and softens 'round the edge
when you offer your best chair;
and, having been made welcome,
loses interest, taking
leave from there.

There were so many bad mornings. Some days the first thought which I considered was deeply personal, relating to either arthritis, or depression. Sigh.

September 4

Chronic.
The word itself sounds
broken with its harsh noise
at beginning and end.

Chronic
is hardly
a death sentence. In a way,
it's really nothing.

No disease at all
somehow
just pain that never ends

but ebbs and flows
with the measure of aspirin
that swims through my veins.

Some days get two poems. This particular bit came on much later in the day, so, really, it's not from under the covers. It's from the dining room.

September 4

In a moment
life is changed
and hope is born.

The car is sold.
There is a check.
I'm ready to go on.

And September 4 goes on. I suspect there was an extended news report on All Things Considered.... Strange, the stuff that gets my mind going, playing with words, with ideas, with rhythm and imagery.

September 4

Syria still looms.
So far away
yet threatening
standing in the room
face to face
a spider in a web
so widely worked
and deeply intertwined
with horror.
We would kill the spider
but dare not
disturb
the web.

A poem of observation.

You'd think that after seven decades
I'd have grown accustomed
to this shell in which
resides my soul.

But it keeps changing:
unlike a chambered nautilus growing
larger and more elegant
as each season passes,

my flesh, my bone, slowly compact,
and twist and swell
and pieces shift
disintegrating on the way.

No longer seeing
what I was, it is
my soul that blooms
in ever clearer light.

It is all that I can hold
that does not fade
nor sputter as life's candle
melts away.

𝒯or good or bad, I am retired, more or less. And mornings grow increasingly difficult. And if I don't have to be up by a certain hour to go to a specific place by some predetermined time....

September 5

> The lump under the covers
> slowly moves and groans
> eyes closed tight against the pain.
>
> Morning has begun.
> She is not yet ready
> to push her way into it.
>
> The covers are thrown off
> only when there is no other way
> to silence the cats.

Yes, I have cats. Down to three now. No, there won't be any more when these finally depart this earth. At least, I don't think so.

*N*ot every morning was a bad one. I hope I always recognize beauty when I see it.

September 6

> I smile.
> The sun is winking at me
> through a hand-worked
> chain of netting
> in the vintage cloth
> that hangs
> in the window.
>
> By the time of
> winter solstice it will
> greet me full face
> directly at my door
> glowing brightly in
> December's crisp
> thin morning.

I don't always remember to say my prayers. But there is something inside me that doesn't want to give voice to a prayer that asks for help. I would like to pray only to offer praise. Which probably isn't very realistic.

September 7

God, please, You're
going to need to yell
a little louder
to wake me from
the self-centered
focus on my own
discomfort.

God, please, don't
hesitate to do what
must be done
to drag me into Your
comforting embrace,
to remind my heart
to sing.

This little book started to exist in my mind months before I signed up with a publisher, or started typing the manuscript. In preparation for my new career as a writer/poet, well, I HAD to have new equipment....

September 8

My new life arrived in boxes.
The laptop - refurbished and repaired
three times and finally perfect.
A printer - sleek and quick,
half the size of the old,
and wireless, magically receiving signals.

Every morning I draw
my poems with a pen,
inscribing a trail of ink
that will be re-imagined
in type, and printed,
published - maybe.

At any rate, the seeds
arrived in boxes. I will
plant them, and watch for
the harvest.

CHAMPAGNE

There should be a label.
Drink only when you are
happy, and deliriously so.

Drink only when mirth abounds,
spangling the air
with drops of joy.

Drink only to celebrate
the new job, the baby, the house,
the wedding.

Don't waste me on your depression.

After yet another bad night....

Not under the covers
but at the table,
tired again
too little sleep
and trying to do
enough about the
house that I can
feel some sense
of accomplishment.

Although,
there is no one
who will care
that I've done
anything
at all.

When I bought the house, it came with an exterminator - sort of. Mike had been treating the house for the previous owner, and I kept up the contract. The first few years were quite an adventure. I believe that at some time in the past a tree had fallen and left a hole in the roof. It was repaired, finally, but the house seems to have spent a couple of years vacant until the owner rented it. Even though that occupant had the exterminator coming every month, his message didn't seem to be getting through to the intended victims.

One morning I had to make a call: I need you NOW. I don't know what it is, but it's sitting in a chair in the living room, and it got dressed in Darth Vader's closet....

September 10

The day's routine
got out of joint
when the
exterminator came.

But how can I start a day
with no poem, with no
thoughtful words to start
the work of life?

September 11

Waking is pinpricks -
little stabs of pain in
shouldersfingerslegs.
Only later, when the
coffee cup is drained
and aspirin on the way
that my pain gives way
to thoughts of others:
A learned friend in hospital
awaiting surgery post crash
even while he oversees the care
of his ageing mother;
the artist friends whose lives
are strictly governed by
the chronic illness of their daughter;
the friend whose life, like mine, is shaped
by ebb and flow of depression's endless cycles,
who cannot always muster a defiant
show of confidence.

I think of them,
feeling guilty that I do so
only after I have quelled
my own distress.

Each day begins
with promise that I don't fulfill.

The dishes get washed
and put away
laundry is done
and always there is
something for the cats.

I eat my meals
tidy the kitchen
make sure my
clothes are washed
and hung

and sometimes there is
energy enough to paint.

How much more energy
does it take
to think of someone else?

I am not the only tired one.

Sleep, or lack thereof, seems to be a normal part of my daily life. I don't know when it started to happen. Certainly there were times in the distant past when emotional stress would keep me awake. Now medication helps me fall asleep, but doesn't keep me from waking halfway through the night. Falling back to sleep means intermittent dozing, with colorful, impossible dreams. I wake for the day - already exhausted.

September 13

Yang and yin.
Black and white.
Yes.
And no.
The balance comes
in opposites.
If I exist
there must be one
somewhere
who sleeps well
wakes fully
and greets the day
feeling alive
ready to meet the world.

Whoever you are
you're welcome.

It's Yom Kippur
the Day of Atonement.
I lie in bed and contemplate the atonement
that becomes a part of me.

The bony frame slowly stiffening
joints overgrown with useless tissue
that freezes fingers into knobby sticks,
skin-covered, still me, but no longer mine.

There is the part that disintegrates
leaving shocked raw bone that grows
again but can manage only to create
a useless, poorly shapen crust.

I wait and daily see myself increasingly imprisoned
by what I thought was mine to master.

I pray for atonement.

I receive a sentence.

The music of Piazzola hit me square in the face on a particular trip to Venice. His 'Oblivion' was played as an encore by Collegium Ducale. I was hooked. A day is suddenly open to the possibility of perfection when I hear Piazzola first thing in the morning. It just doesn't happen often enough.

September 15

Piazzola!
The world is a tango:
the earth rotates
on its axis
to the rhythm of
Buenos Aires
and the seasons sway
summer sliding from
autumn's embrace
to leave the floor
to the flaming color
and seductive grace
of the year's
last dance.

The pen rests in a hand that,
were I to see it in a photograph
I would not know as mine.

In moments when I can redirect my mind
my eye becomes observer -
a scientist - and it's fine.

Change, unpleasant, still amazes.
The child who never noticed growing up
is fascinated now by the ravages of time.

September 17

A poem...
Every day should start
with a poem.
I prove to myself
that I am here
that I am alive
and my brain works
and still I hold a pen
even against the efforts
of the gnarled and swollen
fingers that seek
to cripple me.
I write a poem.

I win.

September 17

September
seems to have just begun
and yet two weeks from now
October will have come.
Days are like pages flying from
a calendar in a film.

I wonder how God sees time.
When it's forever, is there any
difference between one day and the next?
Is one eon any different from another?
Maybe God is still on page one.

Life would be less without the presence of my friend Marilyn. She cared for me after my surgery, and still helps me with grocery shopping. She is an angel. (She would not agree!)

September 18

> Lost in dreaming
> slow to wake
> late to rise
> the day will end
> with nothing done.
>
> (But I *did* make Marilyn laugh)

𝒪nce upon a time I had a houseguest- Italian. It was before I had traveled to Italy myself, and I was unfamiliar with custom. His breakfast every morning was an espresso, and a couple of small cookies, something from Italy he had found at the store. And I am certain that was when the idea began to take shape in my mind.

September 19

It's a morning that needs a cookie - just one.
I don't want breakfast - yes I know it's the
most important meal of the day. But all I really want
is a cookie.
Just a small, buttery biscuit with a bit of chocolate.

They understand cookies in Europe,
making them just large enough
to satisfy the tease of the first bite.
That's all I want with my caffe latte:
to start the day with a tease, and
satisfaction.
And a bit of chocolate.

*N*ews. It keeps happening. Sometimes I wonder why I continue to listen.

September 19

There has been another shooting.
Twelve lie, innocent, but dead.
And officials remain puzzled
questioning the rules, the programs,
the processes that might have
stopped the shooter.

But psychosis will have no master
no schedule of events. The mind,
infinitely powerful, yet balanced
on a blade, will break in its own
mysterious knowledge that
the time is now.

September 20

There IS something:
Izzy had it- Nadia, too.
It's going around.
And it's taunting me:
half an hour at night
just at bedtime
leaving me to wonder
whether I'll sleep
only to reappear in the morning.
I'm almost sneezing.
My throat is almost sore.
I'm almost too tired to get out of bed.
Almost. Almost.
Please just show up already
and let's be done with you!

September 20

The doorway to autumn
the calendar change
has been approaching
from lazy fullness
of summer into
daily brush of color
until the final rush
toward winter's barren cold.

As long as it has been since I could travel to Europe, I haven't stopped dreaming and imagining the possibilities of what could happen. Maybe. Someday.

September 20

It looks as if once again
I'll miss the Orient Express.
It's somewhere
leaving the station
without me in my
velvet and tweed
without my leather suitcase
without the spirit who
makes every moment
an adventure.

Without the tired, crippled woman
who would so love
one last ride.

September 21

After two days
of mercilous teasing
the cold
is here.
Just enough
to wear me down,
to keep the tissues near,
to remind me I need
water, tea;
and quite enough
to spend all afternoon
in bed.

The cats will see to that.

I look and see I've lost
a day or two.
They will be somewhere,
with the torn umbrella
or broken watch
in a box on a shelf
in some half-forgotten hall.

They are somewhere, still.
I've not lost them at all.

September 24

Under the covers
my legs are slim
hips disappear.

I'm not a woman
crippled, old:
just a little child who's cold.

September 24

There is one thing to be said
for growing older:
it is a ride unlike anything
that Disney ever dreamed,
full of twists, turns, drops
that smack you in the face
after a bit of flat track.

Who ever grew old gracefully
when moving depends on a cane,
a walking frame,
when you're trying only
not to fall?

September 25

My grandmother would have called it ugly:
mean people - acting ugly.
But in her day, her day
was there so much ugly?
She left before 9/11
before Mumbai
and Boston
before the ugly of Nairobi
and Afghanistan.
What would she say now?

What is worse than ugly?

The Best Exotic Marigold Hotel
for the Elderly and Beautiful...
I'd go tomorrow if it really did exist,
if Judi and Maggie were there.
The images
float in my mind, the sounds
shimmer in my ears and I
hunger for the color,
the flowing saris
the crowded marketplaces,
the language I don't understand,
the music that makes me dance.

For ten years I have tried to paint
my little world with memories of Venice,
and now Jaipur insinuates itself,
disturbing my complacency,
my quiet life.

Looking up from pen and paper, I'm
stunned by the blandness that looks back.

Time to redecorate.

The elections are coming, elections are coming...and rhetoric has been displaced by tiresome shouting, angry argument. I want no more of it. I have problems enough of my own.

September 26

Perhaps someday there will be
a political party begun by Buddhists.
I could stand fully behind them -
in the middle of the road.

Or, the Puce Party:
no platform, no opinion
only the alliterative reference
to a color long out of fashion.

Nothing worth discussing,
so, perhaps, no anger, no
name calling, no
unpleasant incivility.

Probably too much to ask.

None of this had been planned.
The PLAN had been made years earlier.
I would be frantically active
wearing size six jeans
and four inch heels
my face forever twenty years younger
than the number on my driver's license

and I would meet my end at 89

shot by a jealous wife.

September 27 redux

Waking starts halfway through the night
prelude to a day of pain
and indecision.
Size six is but a dream
and four inch heels have
walked right out of my life.
The face is still young:
it belies a body that
destroys itself from within.
Alone, at the edge of society,
I wait
and wonder how
my life still matters.

Some days just aren't great. It's going to happen: you didn't sleep well, something hurts, the medication doesn't seem to be working, you're feeling depressed. Some days you just accept that it's not the best day you ever had, and do what you can.

September 28

Half the day was spent in bed
feeling none too well
and so there isn't very much
that's left for me to tell.

The dishes went through wash and dry;
all were put away.
Then there was a second load
to finish for the day.

Letters to say thank you,
or, this is how I am.
I'm keeping up, and keeping on
and doing what I can.

Carson mentioned sushi -
its aroma, to be precise,
which made me think,
given the choice,
sashimi would be nice.

In a restaurant panelled
in pale wood
all hand-tooled, neatly joined,
with chopsticks and a sake -
yes, that would be good.

In a lifetime long ago I waited tables in a small traditional Japanese restaurant. I bound myself in kimono, wore tabi and zori, knelt to serve in the tatami rooms. I know how to tie an obi – the real ones, long and in one piece – not the 'cheating' obi that comes in two parts with the final folding already done, to clip into the belt around your waist. It's all beautiful, and very heavy. After nearly three years, putting on the kimono became like getting dressed in 400 years of Japanese history. And don't forget to take small steps: small quick steps.

2003 was an incredible year of success in business, two trips to Venice, and I had lost twenty pounds and was probably as healthy as I would ever be in my life. I know I looked great. There seems to be no photographic evidence to back this up. Sometimes I *do* wish I had the memories confirmed on film.

September 29

> Do I really wish I had more proof
> of who I used to be:
> more photographs or interviews
> with those who knew me when?
>
> Or does my mind hold proof enough
> that I have lived a life: that I was
> young and beautiful
> and danced 'til music's end?

September 30

The day will hold
six loads of laundry,
one of plates -
a visit from a carpenter
scheduling the date
that he will come
to build a wall
behind which I will live,
beginning in the fall.
Soon it's just an alcove
where I'll sleep;
it might be rough,
but small and tidy
just for me -
it will have to be enough.

HOUSEGUESTS

I might could face the day.
It's morning that's the problem.
Half asleep, uncheerful, tired.
Waiting to see the disaster that's
been left behind in the sink.

They collect soiled dishes in their rooms
and bring them all at once;
my good German knives are left sitting,
wet, in the sink; they've no idea how
to load a dishwasher: even the engineer
remains unconvinced that water flows
in a set pattern, and will not wash
what it cannot reach.

Toby Hiram the cat showed up some years back, collarless, but looking perfectly handsome in his black and white tuxedo and black mask. Someone had taken care of him before: he had already been neutered, seemed healthy, and apparently was looking for a new girl friend. I accepted.

October 2

Soundly he sleeps next to me.
In such quiet repose he is so unlike
the killer he sometimes becomes,
devouring prey still warm - fur, bones
and little soul.

He seems such an angel now,
so at peace.
How many souls not his own
have become a part of him?

October 3

Toby had his breakfast
and now demands attention.
Toby is full of morning's meal;
my lap is full of Toby: solid, heavy,
motor running-
prelude to long cold slow
winter dawns
when he'll rather lie asleep,
tucked into me,
than face the chill of the garden
in search of lost chipmunks.

When morning is not Toby,
morning is me:
stiffened body
aching fingers
band of pressure -
invisible diadem -
back that doesn't bend
knees that hurt
joints afire with inflammation
crumbling with degeneration

the slow burn of arthritis.

Can we live a life, and not wonder what happens at the end?

October 5

We grow old
we change
we remain
and wonder
as we go
how many layers
are added
how many
stripped away.

And at the end
will our souls
stand naked
or wrapped
in the dreams
of the lives
we've led?

A friend returned from Germany. Knowing of my interest in food and books, she brought me a charming cookbook in miniature from the region of Saxony.

October 5

A tiny book of recipes
for Saxon cooking
reveals the whole society.

The foods prepared,
 all from the land
they farmed

so closely bound,
each the same:
they were what they ate.

October 6

Lost in time's mists:
Sleep for one night.

If you find it, please
send it back to me.

I will try to hold it
more firmly this time.

A good day?
Of course it will be a good day.

I only spilled half the can
of cat food on the floor;
the oatmeal boiled over,
but only a little bit.
No one bothered to get the trash
and recycling into the bins for pick-up
(but someone *did* remember
to put the bins on the street).

Of course it will be a good day.

Life happens. I survived the day. Again, I win.

October 8

One cannot always go gently
into each new day.

Life happens
and gets in the way
with appointments
and schedules and such.

A morning long in coming
sun slow in rising
caffe latte steaming
is to be desired much.

The covers themselves can inspire a poem...

October 9

Who was the woman - or was it a man -
who first saw the fibers and imagined
the cloth of threads moving over and
under each other forming a plane
that could wrap an infant, or
bind a wound, or grow to a size
that would drape from shoulder
to foot and take the color of wild berries
and precious minerals?

After centuries we think nothing
of the thousands of colors and sizes
of shirts and sheets, blankets and blouses,
folded on shelves, ready to go.
I hope I'm not the only one
who tries to see the first woman weaving,
the first uncertain movements
as she created something that had
never existed before.

October 10

It's seriously autumn.
I stand at the window
counting to ten, and the
falling leaves greatly
outnumber the passing
moments of time.

October 11

If the government can close
then so can I - or very nearly.

Yes, the cats were fed,
and the dishes were washed
and put away.

After a night of little sleep
11 October will not be
a day of great achievement.

But, at the end of the day,
I still am here.
I win.

October 12

I may hurt. Movement
may be awkward,
but I am not helpless.

If I need it I must
get it myself, no matter
how clumsy or uncomfortable.

Because I can, I must.

And so must you. Whatever still moves, however well your body functions, keep working it. Keep walking, pushing, striving – and dreaming.

There now occurs a very long gap, and only one more poem before I would have my hip replacement surgery. The degeneration of the joint had progressed to the movement of my leg bone away from the socket, strain on my lower back, and the accompanying disturbance of surrounding nerves and muscles. I considered myself a cripple, and was spending more and more time in bed because it was so difficult to get up and dress and move.

Maybe you are at that place now. It hurts. It's difficult to imagine yourself old, especially when memories of childhood, school days, first loves, and youthful adventures seem to pop up uncontrollably. You wonder what happened to the person you used to be.

Trust me: you are still there. Your mind is still capable of imagination, your heart is still capable of love, and it is still very much within your power to bring happiness to another. It will take great emotional strength, but it will be there when you need it.

Trust me.

October 23

Morning is colder, darker.
The old window of single-pane glass
is quick to respond to change.
The espresso machine
emits small clouds of
aromatic steam.
I return to my room,
caffe latte in hand,
and see the window
misting with condensate -
late autumn's calling card.

The third week of November 2013, I underwent total hip replacement surgery at Grady Hospital in Atlanta. Doctors and scientists can keep working to make any operation more precise, more safe, more beneficial. But the patient is the one who must recover, and there is no magic pill to make the getting better an overnight process. You will hurt, although it won't be in the same way. You may be too uncomfortable to notice that you can bend your hip without pain. You may feel worse before you feel better. After all, your body has undergone something of an invasion, and needs time to understand all that has happened before it begins to understand that it must heal.

Within 24 hours of my surgery, I was walking with a frame. It was slow, and I would have stayed in bed if I could have! But you have to keep moving. Time will come to meet you, and you will keep walking toward it, and into it. You'll graduate to a rolling walker, or to crutches, and you'll be going a little faster, and you'll be a little less clumsy. And soon you will become impatient to be completely healed, and living life again the way you want to, instead of the way you must.

This manuscript is being finished about thirteen weeks after the Great Day. I now walk through the house on my own, and use a cane only when I'm out and want a bit of security. I imagine that in another two weeks, it's going to stay parked at home. I will be well. Really well. Who knows - maybe I WILL take those tango lessons!

And this will happen for you, whether you are recovering from hip surgery, heart surgery, loss...it will get better. Just keep on walking - toward the future, toward the wellness that you want. Keep your vision focused on it. And if it seems elusive, keep pressing on toward it. Time will move at its own pace, but it will come bringing the healing with it.

And you'll just have to trust me on that one.

...AND THERE'S ONE MORE ->

2014 January 5

The new year begins in the dance
Of new life with new hip,
although real dancing
will come only later.

After six weeks muscles still
are learning to support
the new non-biology of hip,
new posture - no longer falling
over a crumbling joint that once
was femur and acetabulum.

For now, my partner - walking frame -
stands waiting in the corner.
Later we will dance
with the laundry.

Very special thanks are in order for my dear friend, my surrogate son,

Robert Kaleta-Schuetz

who was instrumental in putting the book in order for transmission to the publisher, and in helping me keep my sanity. And thanks for the Imodium.

Made in the USA
Lexington, KY
21 May 2014